THERE'S A
MOUNTAIN
IN THIS
BOOK

MIX
Paper | Supporting
responsible forestry
FSC
www.fsc.org   FSC® C008047

Be the first to know about our new releases,
exclusive content and author events by visiting
thamesandhudson.com
thamesandhudsonusa.com
thamesandhudson.com.au

THERE'S A
MOUNTAIN
IN THIS
BOOK

Rachel Elliot

Illustrated by
Genevieve Lacroix

CONTENTS

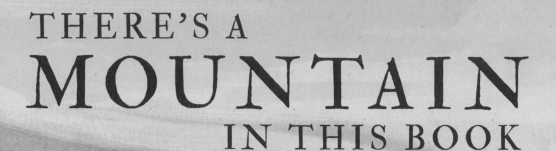

THERE'S A MOUNTAIN IN THIS BOOK

WELCOME TO
BASECAMP
FEARLESS EXPLORER!

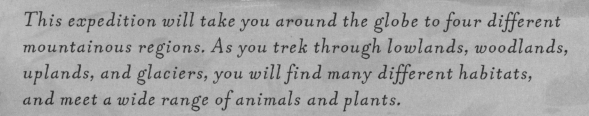

This expedition will take you around the globe to four different mountainous regions. As you trek through lowlands, woodlands, uplands, and glaciers, you will find many different habitats, and meet a wide range of animals and plants.

A mountain is not just a giant lump of rock: it is also an interconnected ecosystem bursting with life, from tiny beetles to towering trees and mighty bears. An ecosystem is a place where the landscape, plants, animals, and weather work together to make a bubble of life. Just as a busy town is filled with a variety of buildings and people, an ecosystem contains many habitats where lots of different plants and animals live.

Your mission is to explore mountain environments. Notice everything! Collect samples and draw pictures. Write notes about the things you find. By the time you have reached the summit of each mountain, you will have filled your expedition journal with adventures.

THE MOUNTAIN CODE

LEAVE NO TRACE

1. Plan your expedition carefully.
2. Walk and camp on sturdy ground.
3. Leave all places as you find them.
4. Respect wildlife.
5. Be considerate.
6. Don't litter.

WHAT MAKES A GOOD EXPLORER?

BELIEF that your mission will succeed.

PATIENCE. Nature takes its time.

KINDNESS to animals and people.

COURAGE to keep going.

ORGANIZATION so you are well prepared.

IMAGINATION to solve problems.

NEVER GIVE UP!

MOUNTAIN
ZONES

You are almost ready to begin your journey. Wonderful adventures lie ahead among rolling foothills, towering forests, alpine uplands, and snowy peaks. These four different zones can be found in most mountain environments.

The temperature gets colder as you climb higher. That is why you will see different plants and animals in each zone.

SNOWY PEAKS

Among the majestic peaks you will face glaciers, vertical cliffs, and sudden storms. Your path leads past the highest villages to the snow zone, where few plants or animals can survive.

ALPINE UPLANDS

Here, it is too cold and windy for trees to survive. But life finds a way! Grasses, shrubs, mosses, and lichens flourish between the treeline and the snow line. You may even find towns and villages this high up!

CONIFER FOREST

Evergreen woodlands tower over the next zone. Some animals and plants cannot survive in this colder environment, so the ecosystem here is less varied.

FOOTHILLS

A mountain's lower slopes and valleys are called the foothills. They are teeming with life! You will trek through woodland bursting with plants, trees, and animals.

HOW IS A MOUNTAIN MADE?

FOLD MOUNTAIN

FOLD MOUNTAIN

Do you like jigsaw puzzles? Earth's surface (the crust) is made of big slabs called tectonic plates. They fit together like a puzzle. When two of the plates crash together, the rocks crumple upward, just as a flat piece of paper crumples when it's scrunched up.

Sediment and some magma is forced upwards

Deep mountain roots

PLATE MOVEMENT

PLATE MOVEMENT

Magma

River

DID YOU KNOW?

If you could fold a piece of paper 27 times, it would be taller than Mount Everest!

PLATEAU MOUNTAIN

DOME MOUNTAIN

HOW IS A MOUNTAIN MADE?

Not all mountains are the same. OK, they're big and hard to climb, but there is more than one way to make one. Most mountains are created when something happens inside the Earth to push rocks upward.

PRESSURE

Magma

PLATEAU MOUNTAIN

Slowly but surely, water wears rock down. Rivers carve deep channels into rock. In time, these become valleys with mountains on either side.

DOME MOUNTAIN

When magma doesn't break through the Earth's crust, it makes it bulge upward in a dome shape. The magma cools and hardens into rock.

River

You are traveling to four unforgettable locations:

NORTH AMERICA

The Rocky Mountains are around 80 million years old. There are many wonders to see here, from massive sand dunes to dangerous glaciers, and a supervolcano.

EUROPE

The Alps are the highest mountain range in Western Europe. They cover about 80,000 square miles and spread across eight countries: Monaco, France, Italy, Switzerland, Liechtenstein, Germany, Austria, and Slovenia.

The Rocky Mountains

The Alps

The Himalayas

Mount Kilimanjaro

AFRICA

Kilimanjaro is the highest mountain in Africa. It is 19,340 feet tall. That's like 1,000 giraffes standing on top of each other!

ASIA

Over 53 million people call the Himalayas home. It is here that you will find the highest mountain in the world—Mount Everest. Only the strongest and bravest explorers venture up to the peak. This is the final ecosystem you will visit, and your toughest challenge!

WHAT IS AN ECOSYSTEM?

Many animals and plants live alongside each other on these mountains. The word ecosystem describes how they are all connected. Every living and non-living thing in an ecosystem has a part to play. This includes plants and animals as well as things like water, rocks, and soil.

This might sound like a silly question, but ... what is a mountain? Before we set off, it's important to understand the places you'll be exploring.

A mountain is an area of land that rises high above the surrounding landscape. Mountains often have steep sides called slopes, which are broken up into a series of ridges and peaks, leading up to the highest point: the summit. There are mountains on every continent and even under the sea.

DID YOU KNOW?

Mountains are rarely found on their own. They are usually linked together in mountain ranges, which can be thousands of miles long. Mountain ranges themselves are often interconnected, forming a mountain system.

EXPEDITION AIMS:

- To learn more about the mountain ecosystem.
- To place our expedition flag at the summit.
- To have an adventure!

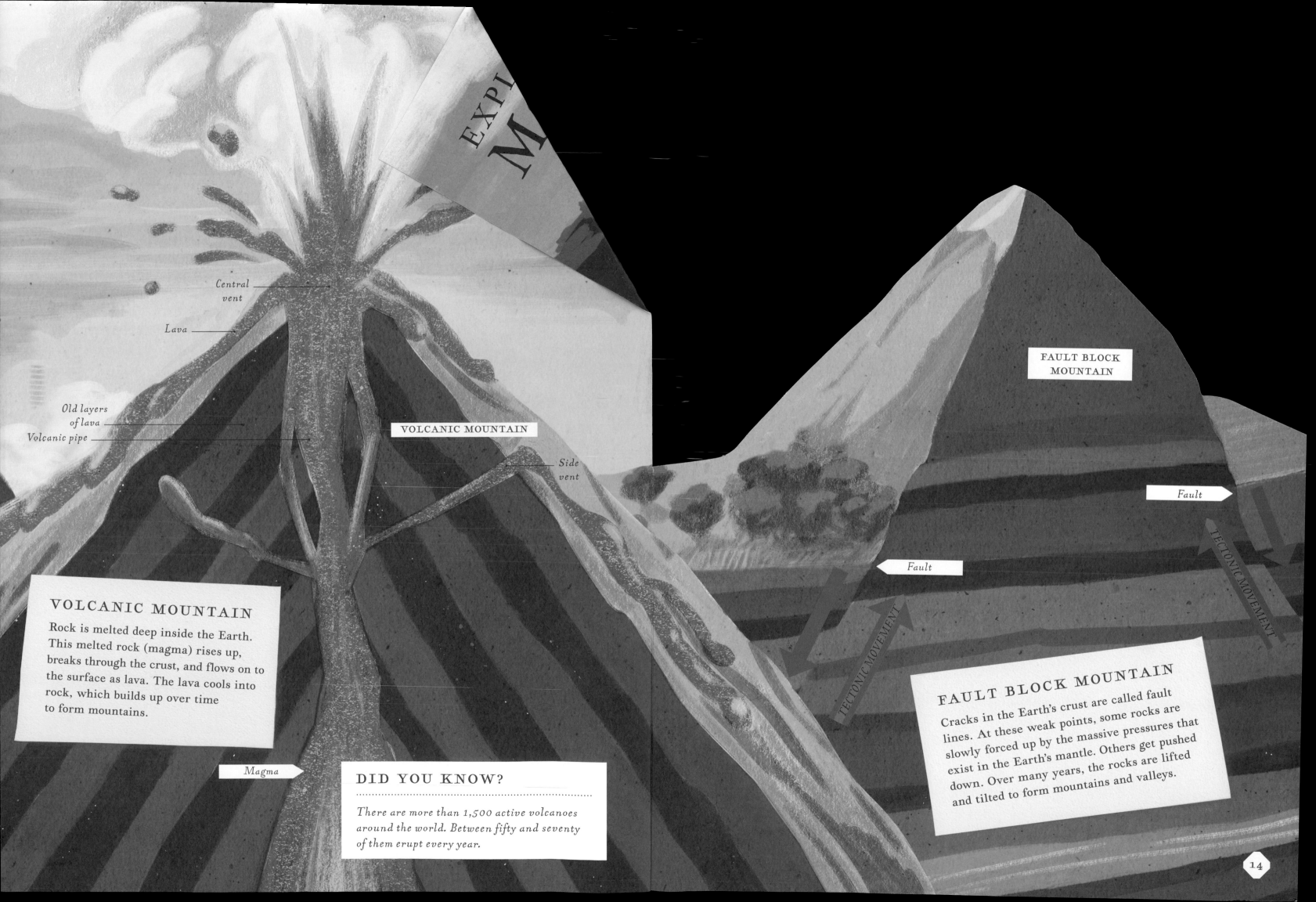

EXPI
M

Central
vent

Lava

FAULT BLOCK
MOUNTAIN

Old layers
of lava

Volcanic pipe

VOLCANIC MOUNTAIN

Side
vent

Fault

TECTONIC MOVEMENT

Fault

TECTONIC MOVEMENT

VOLCANIC MOUNTAIN

Rock is melted deep inside the Earth.
This melted rock (magma) rises up,
breaks through the crust, and flows on to
the surface as lava. The lava cools into
rock, which builds up over time
to form mountains.

Magma

DID YOU KNOW?

*There are more than 1,500 active volcanoes
around the world. Between fifty and seventy
of them erupt every year.*

FAULT BLOCK MOUNTAIN

Cracks in the Earth's crust are called fault
lines. At these weak points, some rocks are
slowly forced up by the massive pressures that
exist in the Earth's mantle. Others get pushed
down. Over many years, the rocks are lifted
and tilted to form mountains and valleys.

HOW HIGH IS HIGH?

The distance from the base of a mountain to the summit tells us how tall the whole mountain is. A mountain's height measures how far away it is from sea level. The highest mountain above sea level is Mount Everest. The tallest mountain is Mauna Kea, on Hawaii.

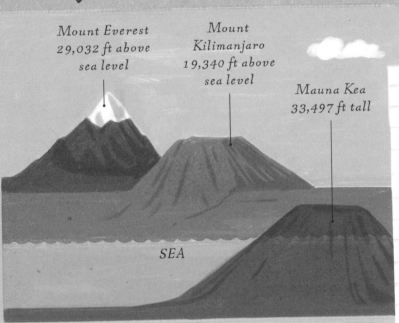

Mount Everest
29,032 ft above
sea level

Mount Kilimanjaro
19,340 ft above
sea level

Mauna Kea
33,497 ft tall

SEA

HOW HEAVY IS A MOUNTAIN?

The average mountain weighs millions of tons. There are no scales big enough to pop a mountain on, but the estimated weight of Mount Everest is 175 billion tons. That's roughly the same weight as 25 billion elephants!

HOW LONG IS LONG?

The longest mountain system is called the mid-ocean ridge. It's a whopping 132,513 ft long. That means it could go one and a half times around the Earth! About 90 per cent of it is under the Atlantic Ocean. The only part above sea level is in Iceland. The longest mountain range above grounds is the Andes, which is about 18,143 ft long.

...LORING
...OUNTAINS

FLYING
To get a bird's-eye view, you could try a hang glider. These aircraft have no engines. Instead, the pilot uses their body weight to control the flight.

CLIMBING
Climbers use their strength and determination to get to places that hikers can't reach. They have ropes and special equipment to help them.

BOATING
Some mountain lakes are perfect for water sports. Skilled sailors explore creeks and coves against a backdrop of snowy peaks. You might see sailing boats, paddle boards, canoes, and pedal boats on the turquoise water.

HIKING
Traveling on foot allows hikers to take their time on the mountain. They enjoy feeling the ground beneath their feet and connecting with their surroundings. They are fit and well prepared for whatever might happen.

EXPLORING
MOUNTAINS

FLYING
To get a bird's-eye view,
you could try a hang glider.
These aircraft have no engines.
Instead, the pilot uses their
body weight to control the flight.

CLIMBING
Climbers use their strength and
determination to get to places that
hikers can't reach. They have ropes
and special equipment to help them.

BOATING
Some mountain lakes are perfect for water
sports. Skilled sailors explore creeks and coves
against a backdrop of snowy peaks. You might
see sailing boats, paddle boards, canoes,
and pedal boats on the turquoise water.

HIKING
Traveling on foot allows hikers to take their
time on the mountain. They enjoy feeling
the ground beneath their feet and connecting
with their surroundings. They are fit and
well prepared for whatever might happen.

Ash cloud

Central
vent

Lava

Old layers
of lava

Volcanic pipe

VOLCANIC MOUNTAIN

Si
ve

VOLCANIC MOUNTAIN

Rock is melted deep inside the Earth.
This melted rock (magma) rises up,
breaks through the crust, and flows on to
the surface as lava. The lava cools into
rock, which builds up over time
to form mountains.

Magma

DID YOU KNOW?

There are more than 1,500 active volca
around the world. Between fifty and sev
of them erupt every year.

HOW HIGH IS HIGH?

The distance from the base of a mountain to the summit tells us how tall the whole mountain is. A mountain's height measures how far away it is from sea level. The highest mountain above sea level is Mount Everest. The tallest mountain is Mauna Kea, on Hawaii.

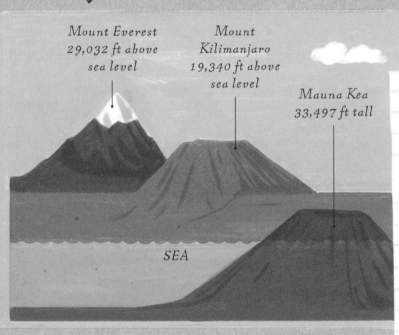

Mount Everest 29,032 ft above sea level

Mount Kilimanjaro 19,340 ft above sea level

Mauna Kea 33,497 ft tall

SEA

HOW HEAVY IS A MOUNTAIN?

The average mountain weighs millions of tons. There are no scales big enough to pop a mountain on, but the estimated weight of Mount Everest is 175 billion tons. That's roughly the same weight as 25 billion elephants!

HOW LONG IS LONG?

The longest mountain system is called the mid-ocean ridge. It's a whopping 132,513 ft long. That means it could go one and a half times around the Earth! About 90 per cent of it is under the Atlantic Ocean. The only part above sea level is in Iceland. The longest mountain range above ground is the Andes, which is about 18,143 ft long.

EXPLORING MOUNTAINS

FLYING

To get a bird's-eye view, you could try a hang glider. These aircraft have no engines. Instead, the pilot uses their body weight to control the flight.

CLIMBING

Climbers use their strength and determination to get to places that hikers can't reach. They have ropes and special equipment to help them.

BOATING

Some mountain lakes are perfect for water sports. Skilled sailors explore creeks and coves against a backdrop of snowy peaks. You might see sailing boats, paddle boards, canoes, and pedal boats on the turquoise water.

HIKING

Traveling on foot allows hikers to take their time on the mountain. They enjoy feeling the ground beneath their feet and connecting with their surroundings. They are fit and well prepared for whatever might happen.

Human beings have been exploring mountains for hundreds of years. Nowadays, there are lots of exciting ways to experience these beautiful places. People challenge themselves and their bodies to see nature from a new angle.

Some mountain sports make you feel as if it's just you and the mountain. Others are more fun with friends. What would you like to try?

⚠ MOUNTAIN WEATHER CHANGES QUICKLY. IT CAN BECOME DANGEROUS IN JUST A FEW MINUTES, SO STAY ALERT!

SKIING
Skiers attach long strips of wood, metal, or plastic to their feet and slide over the snow. It takes great skill and lots of practice.

CYCLING
Mountain bikes are a fun way to travel through fields and forests, up slopes, and past lakes. There are plenty of places to stop for food and drink along the way!

TO DO:
- Be prepared for temperature changes.
- Research local wildlife.
- Pack a map and a compass.
- Remember a first aid kit.

17

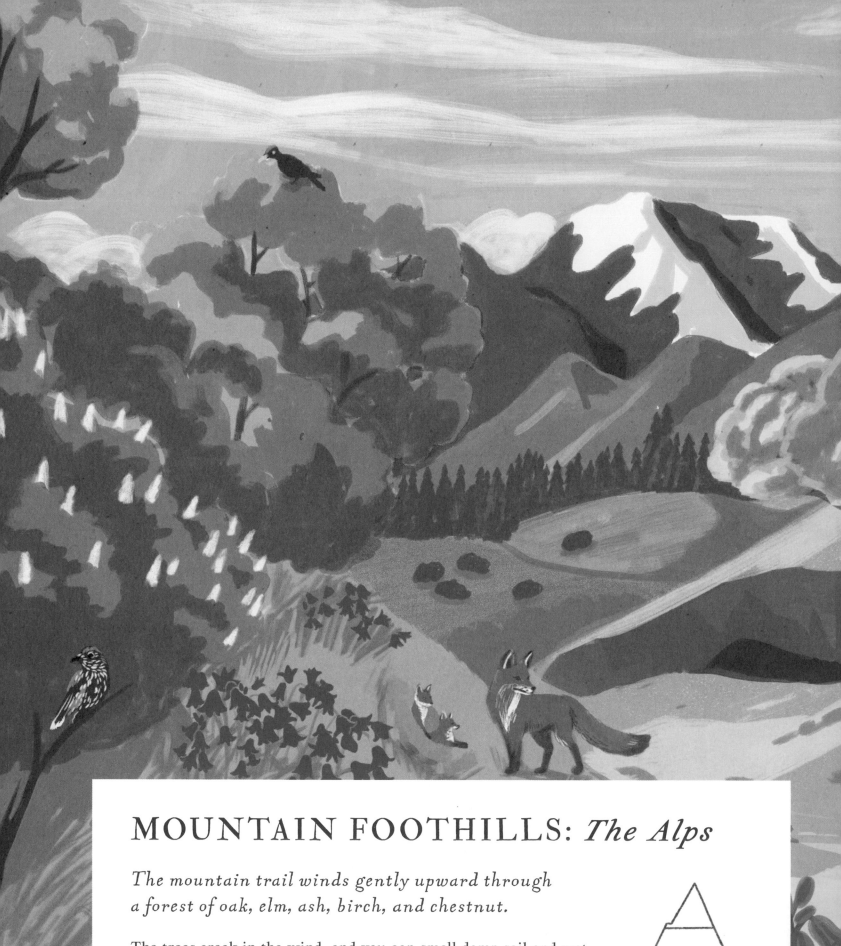

MOUNTAIN FOOTHILLS: *The Alps*

The mountain trail winds gently upward through a forest of oak, elm, ash, birch, and chestnut.

The trees creak in the wind, and you can smell damp soil and wet bark. Somewhere nearby, a bear is roaring. Eagles soar overhead and birdsong fills the air. Is that the rustle of leaves? No, it's a mountain fox scurrying through the shady undergrowth. Are you curious enough to find out what lives inside the woods?

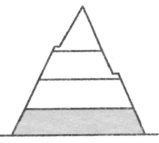

Foothills

30,000 ft

25,000 ft

20,000 ft

15,000 ft

10,000 ft

5,000 ft

0 ft

THE FOOTHILLS

BLACK WOODPECKER

WINGSPAN: 25-33 in.
FAVORITE SNACKS: ants,
insect larvae, berries, dried fruit.
SONG: a ringing call of "kuii, kuii, kuii."
BEST FEATURE: it wraps its long,
sticky tongue around its skull
when it's not in use.

The LIME TREE has sweet,
yellow-white flowers and
little, round seeds that
float away on the wind.

GOLDEN EAGLE

WINGSPAN: 71-92 in.
FAVORITE SNACKS: marmots,
squirrels, hares, rabbits.
TOP SPEED: 124 miles per hour.
BEST FEATURE: incredible eyesight.
They can spot prey 1 km away!

BROWN BEAR

SIZE: Up to 87 in.
FAVORITE SNACKS: deer,
fish, berries, honey, nuts.
FUN FACT: bears have to
eat about 20,000 calories
each day to prepare for
hibernation. That's about
200 apples!

HAREBELLS are known by
many names, including
witches' thimbles, small
bluebells, and fairy bells.

THROUGH *the* FOREST

Don't move! A few yards away, a big, brown bear shuffles over to a dead tree. He has sniffed out something tasty. Bees buzz around him, but he doesn't care. It's worth getting a few stings to taste their yummy honey!

In winter, skiers will swish down these green slopes. Now, hikers and mountain bikers share the winding pathways with animals, from rabbits and hares to wolves and vipers.

The lowlands are dotted with wild mushrooms. The air is full of their rich, earthy smell. People fill their baskets with edible fungi—if the boars haven't gobbled them up first.

FORAGING NOTES

1. If you cannot confidently identify a plant, don't eat it.

2. Many mushrooms are edible, but they can be hard to correctly identify because they look very similar to poisonous ones. So, only go foraging if you're with an expert!

A hawthorn bush quivers and two big, black eyes blink shyly at you. It is a reddish-brown roe deer. For a moment, she freezes. Then she bounds away, her white rump bobbing through the trees. Where is she going?

A HAPPY COMEBACK

In the past, some animals were hunted so much that they disappeared from the Alps. Recently, wolves, lynx, ibex, vultures, and brown bears have been brought back to the mountains and their numbers are growing.

30,000 ft

25,000 ft

20,000 ft

15,000 ft

10,000 ft

5,000 ft

0 ft

INTO *the* CAVE

You push through the thick undergrowth, your feet squelching in earthy mulch. Here, the forest floor is bursting with life. Beetles and bugs creep and buzz among plants and flowers. Ahead is the entrance to a cave. You crawl into a dark tunnel, looking for adventure.

ALPINE LONGHORN BEETLE

A lucky sighting of the rarely seen Alpine longhorn beetle!

FOSSILS

Many fossils have been found inside the cave, including cave lions and leopards. They are hundreds of thousands of years old.

Cave lion skull

30,000 ft

25,000 ft

20,000 ft

15,000 ft

10,000 ft

5,000 ft

0 ft

There are creatures in these caves that have never seen the sun. They have evolved without eyes or color. They use their sensitive hearing, touch, and taste to find food.

TROGLOBITES

OLM

The cave opens into a huge, echoing cavern. Fragile stalactites hang from the roof like crystal straws. Drips of water plop into a vast underground lake.

Troglobites are animals that have adapted to living in caves, like these spiders, pseudoscorpions, and shrimp. Ecosystems can be big or small. A mountain is a huge ecosystem, but the space under a rock is an ecosystem too.

The olm is the only amphibian in Europe that lives in caves. It eats, sleeps, and breeds underwater. It can live for up to 100 years!

CONIFER FOREST: *The Rocky Mountains*

A sweet scent makes you stop and sniff the air.
Flat-topped ponderosa pines surround you, and
their bark smells like vanilla. You are tramping
through the conifer forests of the Rocky Mountains.

This is a cooler zone, where the trees stay green all year round.
Rivers curve around meadows of wildflowers. Grasses and
shrubs grow between the tall, straight pine trees.

Conifer forest

Millions of tourists visit the area's national parks each year for activities like
camping, fishing, hunting, and mountain biking. The Rocky Mountains (or Rockies)
form the largest mountain range in North America. The sheer size takes your breath
away. It is as if you're the only one here.

For thousands of years, people
and animals have sheltered in
this cave. There are fossils
in the rock layers, but life
can still be found inside.

THE CONIFER FOREST

YELLOW-RUMPED WARBLER

Spotted skimming insects from the river's surface

MOURNING CLOAK BUTTERFLY

Spotted resting on a branch

SNOWSHOE HARE

spotted nibbling a fern

MARMOT

Spotted peeping out of a burrow

OLD FAITHFUL

Yellowstone National Park is part of the Rockies. It's home to over 500 geysers, including the mighty "Old Faithful." A geyser is a special type of spring that shoots hot water from underground into the air like a fountain. At predictable times throughout the day, Old Faithful blasts a stream of boiling water to a height of around 144 ft.

30,000 ft

25,000 ft

20,000 ft

15,000 ft

10,000 ft

5,000 ft

0 ft

You gaze up at a slope ahead and notice that
one side is covered in a dense, dark forest
of Douglas fir and Colorado blue spruce.
North-facing slopes get less sun throughout
the day. This keeps the soil cooler and moister,
causing more trees to grow closer together.

Clinging to the rocky
ledge, a limber pine has
been gnarled and twisted
into fantastical shapes by
the wind. As you watch,
a porcupine waddles up
to nibble its pinkish bark.

ABOVE *the* CANYON

You reach a ledge and stop to rest, looking down into a deep canyon. Pine-covered slopes rise and fall as far as you can see and the sun is warm.

Canyons are made in a variety of ways. The most common are river canyons, which form as the river's water gradually carves a path down through the rock. They can take millions of years to form.

PORCUPINE

Thanks to their sharp claws, porcupines are skilful climbers. They build their dens inside rock crevices or hollow trees.

CALLIOPE HUMMINGBIRD

You can easily recognize a male by his magenta throat feathers. This is the smallest bird in the United States: about the same size as a ping-pong ball!

SNEEZEWEED

When crushed to a powder, these yellow flowers can make you sneeze.

30,000 ft

25,000 ft

20,000 ft

15,000 ft

10,000ft

5,000 ft

0 ft

ON *the* LAKE

At the edge of the forest, you reach a crystal-clear lake. Dense canopies of tall, straight lodgepole pine are reflected in the glassy water. Under its shimmering surface, this lake is full of life.

Everything in an ecosystem exists in a delicate balance. If something disturbs that balance, the ecosystem changes. Imagine a lake at the heart of an ecosystem. Lots of plants and animals rely on the water to keep them alive. If the water is polluted, those plants and animals will die. It's important to keep our planet healthy and fight pollution.

In this zone, plants protect themselves from the weather by staying close to the ground. Over time, some of the animals have changed to cope with the cold conditions and the extreme sunlight. Others hibernate, or leave during the worst weather.

ALPINE ADAPTORS

Alpine animals are great problem solvers! On mountains across the world, they have adapted to live in this harsh environment in different ways.

PROBLEM: cold weather.
SOLUTION: layers of fat; shorter legs, tails, and ears to reduce heat loss.

PROBLEM: strong sunlight.
SOLUTION: thick fur to protect the skin.

PROBLEM: less oxygen.
SOLUTION: larger lungs, more blood cells.

GIANT GROUNDSEL

These alien-looking plants are found on mountains in Africa. This particular type is only found here on Kilimanjaro. They store water in their stems, and their leaves close when the temperature gets too cold.

SCARLET-TUFTED SUNBIRD

This dazzling bird uses its long beak to reach the nectar inside giant lobelias.

GIANT LOBELIA

Tall giant lobelias have developed to survive frosty nights. A single plant can hold several gallons of water.

FOUR-STRIPED GRASS MOUSE

These little survivors can live without water as long as there is some in their food. They dig a network of burrows and hide the entrances among plants.

10000m
9000m
8000m
7000m
6000m
5000m
4000m
3000m
2000m
1000m
0m

ALPINE CHAT

This songbird is brave and curious about people. It may approach you to investigate!

MOUNTAIN BUZZARD

This bird of prey nests in the forest, but flies to higher zones to search for rodent snacks.

ROCK HYRAX

Among crevices in the rocks, perhaps you will see one of these rare mammals. Look out for their long, pointed teeth like tusks. They are distant relatives of the elephant!

SNOWY PEAKS: *The Himalayas*

You are getting closer to the snowy summit.
Even though the sun is shining, the temperature
is below freezing. You're wearing lots of layers!

A few shrubs and boulders are studded across the snowy landscape.
The permanent snow line is very close. A small family of blue
sheep crosses your path. They must be looking for herbs or
shrubs. They leap nimbly onto the rocks around you. A lone
bearded vulture soars through the shimmering blue sky.

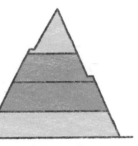

Snowy peaks

MOORLANDS AND ALPINE DESERT

After the shade of the rainforest, it is hard to find shelter from the sun. This is a harsh place for living things, and very few animals live this high up. Before you reach the snow line, your path leads you over clumps of grass, heather, and scrubby shrubs. It's windy and cold, and yet the sun beats down relentlessly.

The ground is rocky and Kilimanjaro's largest peak, Kibo, towers above you. There is still a long way to go! Ahead lies a high desert of volcanic dust. Not even moss grows there, and only a few insects still survive.

This is the hardest part of your journey so far. At this height the air contains much less oxygen than normal. This causes some people to feel sick and get headaches as their body finds it difficult to work with reduced oxygen. This is called altitude sickness.

At this height, no one can walk as quickly as before. You rest often, letting your body get used to the thinner air. Larger animals from the forest rarely come up this high. You glimpse a few birds and insects. Rodents scurry over pebbles and stones, or burrow into the sun-dried ground.

IF YOU GET ALTITUDE SICKNESS:
- Stop and rest.
- Drink plenty of water.
- Don't climb any higher for at least two days.

Shh! A mountain lion is prowling by the water's edge. It crouches, ready to pounce, staring through the tall grass. Has it seen a rabbit, or a deer? Or is it going to risk attacking a bighorn sheep?

30,000 ft

25,000 ft

20,000 ft

15,000 ft

10,000 ft

5,000 ft

0 ft

GRAND PRISMATIC SPRING

This hot spring in Yellowstone National Park is famous for its incredible colors. Bacteria around the edges of the water make colorful pigments that turn the area red, orange, yellow, green, and blue.

BIGHORN SHEEP

Have you ever stood face to face with a bighorn ram? They are the largest wild sheep in North America and can grow to over 3 ft tall and weigh over 2 lbs. You wouldn't want to be butted by those horns!

RAINFOREST ADVENTURE

You have been hiking through Kilimanjaro's rainforest zone. Till now, the trail has been filled with beautiful orchids, tiny lizards, and lush trees covered with "old man's beard" lichen. Suddenly you glimpse the mighty summit of Kilimanjaro, framed by leaves. It is a breathtaking sight.

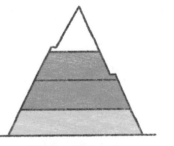

Alpine Uplands

Suddenly, something amazing happens.
A majestic snow leopard lopes into sight and lies
down to bask in the sun. Its color and fur pattern
camouflage it against the rocks.
This beautiful animal is rarely
seen, so you are very lucky.

SNOW LEOPARD

Snow leopards have big paws that are covered in fur to help them walk across snow.

BEARDED VULTURE

These vultures are scavengers that feed on the remains of dead animals. Up to 90 per cent of their diet is just bones!

SIGNS THAT A SNOW LEOPARD MAY BE NEARBY:

- Pugmarks: paw prints in the snow.
- Scrapes: heart-shaped scuffs in the ground with a pile of earth at one end.
- Scats: snow leopard poop.
- Claw rakes: scratches on rocks.

WHAT IS THE PERMANENT SNOW LINE?

On some parts of a mountain, there will only be snow at certain times of the year. However, above a certain height, you will find snow all year. This is called the permanent snow line.

NORTH FACING

Permanent snow line

SOUTH FACING

30,000 ft

25,000 ft

20,000 ft

15,000 ft

10,000 ft

5,000 ft

0 ft

You reach a massive icefall.
Ropes are there to help you across,
and narrow ladders bridge deep
cracks, or crevasses, in the ice.
Stay alert for falling rocks
and unstable ice!

ICEFALL

HIMALAYAN
JUMPING SPIDER

GLACIER

30,000 ft

25,000 ft

20,000 ft

15,000 ft

10,000 ft

5,000 ft

0 ft

THROUGH ICE *and* SNOW

The weather has changed. Snow is falling heavily and the sun has disappeared. All you can hear is the roar of the biting wind. You just keep putting one foot in front of the other.

There are no plants here, although you have spotted a few small patches of moss. The only sign of animal life is a tiny spider scurrying among the rocks.

A fierce wall of wind blows you to your knees. You push yourself up and inch forward, leaning into the wind. This is the hardest trek you have ever done.

WHAT IS A GLACIER?

A glacier is like a river of ice. Gravity makes it move downward, but very, very slowly! Glaciers are made when snow falls in one place for many years without melting. The old snow at the bottom gets squashed down by the weight and turns to ice.

WHAT IS AN ICEFALL?

SERAC

CREVASSE

Icefalls happen when the ice in one part of a glacier flows faster than the rest. The ice breaks up, making deep cracks (crevasses) and ice towers (seracs).

HOW TO WALK IN HARD SNOW

1. Wear crampons—special spikes you can attach to your shoes.

2. To walk up a slope, keep your feet straight, and bend your knees.

3. To walk down, take small steps, and make sure that your whole sole meets the ground.

HOW TO WALK IN LOOSE SNOW

1. To walk up a slope, kick the snow with your toe, and go up as if you were climbing a flight of stairs.

2. If you sink into the snow, don't panic. Lean on your pole and take another step.

3. To go down, dig your heel into the snow, and put your weight on it. Slide downward until your foot feels stable.

BAR-HEADED GOOSE

This goose is one of the highest flying birds in the world. It crosses over some of the highest peaks of the Himalayas during its yearly migration.

AT *the* SUMMIT

Using ropes, you climb steadily up a steep rock toward a ridge. There is a sheer drop to the valley below. Stones and ice crash down from the end of the glacier, making a dusty haze.

The deep, snow-covered ridge leads into the clouds. You make your way slowly along the trail, until the clouds part and you see some of the tallest peaks on the planet. You have reached the summit!

You breathe in the cold, fresh scent of mountain snow and gaze at the white wilderness. The rays of the setting sun touch the peaks and turn them from white to red and orange.

30,000 ft

25,000 ft

20,000 ft

15,000 ft

10,000 ft

5,000 ft

0 ft

HOW'S THE WEATHER UP THERE?

The climate and weather of a mountain are affected by many things. Climate is the average weather over many years. Weather is a particular event, like a snowstorm or a windy day. It can happen over hours, days, or weeks.

WET WEATHER

Mountains are wetter places than lower lands. Warm winds carry moisture across the land and rise up over the mountain. The air cools as it rises, and because cool air can't carry as much moisture, it falls as rain. Often the windward side of a mountain gets more rain than the leeward side. The area of land with less rain is called a rain shadow, and it can become a desert if there is almost no rain.

WIND WORDS

- Prevailing winds always blow in the same direction.
- The windward side of a mountain faces the wind.
- The leeward side of a mountain is protected from the wind.

Shh! A mountain lion is prowling by the water's edge. It crouches, ready to pounce, staring through the tall grass. Has it seen a rabbit, or a deer? Or is it going to risk attacking a bighorn sheep?

GRAND PRISMATIC SPRING

This hot spring in Yellowstone National Park is famous for its incredible colors. Bacteria around the edges of the water make colorful pigments that turn the area red, orange, yellow, green, and blue.

BIGHORN SHEEP

Have you ever stood face to face with a bighorn ram? They are the largest wild sheep in North America and can grow to over 3 ft tall and weigh over 2 lbs. You wouldn't want to be butted by those horns!

30,000 ft

25,000 ft

20,000 ft

15,000 ft

10,000 ft

5,000 ft

0 ft

RAINFOREST ADVENTURE

You have been hiking through Kilimanjaro's rainforest zone. Till now, the trail has been filled with beautiful orchids, tiny lizards, and lush trees covered with "old man's beard" lichen. Suddenly you glimpse the mighty summit of Kilimanjaro, framed by leaves. It is a breathtaking sight.

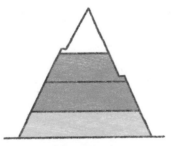

Alpine Uplands

CLIMBING CALENDAR

The weather on a mountain can change dramatically depending on the seasons. This means that it is often easier and safer to climb certain mountains at particular times of the year. For example, in summer, the Indian Himalayas face monsoon weather, which means there is a lot of very heavy rain. Spring or autumn is a good time to visit instead. However, the Andes in Peru should be tackled in summer, when the weather is usually dry.

Whatever the season, the weather on a mountain can be extreme. Some mountain ranges, like the central Andes, seem to have only two seasons — rainy and dry!

JANUARY

ACONCAGUA, ARGENTINA
*The highest mountain
in the Americas.*

MAY

INCA TRAIL, PERU
*This trek will lead you to the
"lost city" of Machu Picchu, built
by the Inca people 600 years ago.*

SEPTEMBER

KHAN TENGRI, KAZAKHSTAN
*Sometimes called "Blood Mountain"
because its marble peak often
glows red at sunset.*

RAINBOW MOUNTAIN

Vinicunca is an unusual mountain in the central Andes of Peru that is famous for its colorful stripes. The rainbow effect is caused by different minerals in the rock. Vinicunca is best climbed during the dry season, between May and October.

WHY ARE MOUNTAINS COLDEST AT THE TOP?

The climate at the top of a mountain is different from the climate at the bottom. The higher the altitude, the thinner the air. Thin air can't trap as much heat, so the further up you go, the colder it will be.

SPOTTERS GUIDE TO CLOUDS

There are lots of different types of cloud that form at higher altitudes. Some of them look truly awesome. Keep a lookout for all of these:

CIRRUS

CIRROCUMULUS

CIRROSTRATUS

LENTICULAR

KELVIN-HELMHOLTZ

HOW IS CLIMATE CHANGE AFFECTING MOUNTAINS?

Over time, the world is getting warmer. Many mountain ecosystems are noticing the effects of this climate change. As temperatures rise, there is less snow. Most mountain-dwelling species have moved higher to live in cooler areas and find their favorite food. But as they move up the mountain, the area they live in gets smaller.

SNOW FACTS

Did you know that all rain starts as snow? It melts while its falling. But on high mountain peaks, it lands before it melts.

- A single snowflake contains about 200 ice crystals.
- All snowflakes have six sides or arms.
- No two snowflakes are exactly the same.
- Snow isn't white! It's actually see-through.

DID YOU KNOW?

···

The weather on a mountain is often unpredictable and can change dramatically in minutes.

HOW TO WALK IN HARD SNOW

1. Wear crampons—special spikes you can attach to your shoes.

2. To walk up a slope, keep your feet straight, and bend your knees.

3. To walk down, take small steps, and make sure that your whole sole meets the ground.

HOW TO WALK IN LOOSE SNOW

1. To walk up a slope, kick the snow with your toe, and go up as if you were climbing a flight of stairs.

2. If you sink into the snow, don't panic. Lean on your pole and take another step.

3. To go down, dig your heel into the snow, and put your weight on it. Slide downward until your foot feels stable.

BAR-HEADED GOOSE

This goose is one of the highest flying birds in the world. It crosses over some of the highest peaks of the Himalayas during its yearly migration.

GLACIER

30,000 ft

25,000 ft

20,000 ft

15,000 ft

10,000 ft

5,000 ft

0 ft

THROUGH ICE *and* SNOW

The weather has changed. Snow is falling heavily and the sun has disappeared. All you can hear is the roar of the biting wind. You just keep putting one foot in front of the other.

There are no plants here, although you have spotted a few small patches of moss. The only sign of animal life is a tiny spider scurrying among the rocks.

A fierce wall of wind blows you to your knees. You push yourself up and inch forward, leaning into the wind. This is the hardest trek you have ever done.

WHAT IS A GLACIER?

A glacier is like a river of ice. Gravity makes it move downward, but very, very slowly! Glaciers are made when snow falls in one place for many years without melting. The old snow at the bottom gets squashed down by the weight and turns to ice.

WHAT IS AN ICEFALL?

SERAC

CREVASSE

Icefalls happen when the ice in one part of a glacier flows faster than the rest. The ice breaks up, making deep cracks (crevasses) and ice towers (seracs).

TIME TO CLIMB

This mountain calendar will help you to plan your next adventure.

FEBRUARY

KILIMANJARO, TANZANIA
The world's tallest free-standing mountain.

MARCH

OJOS DEL SALADO, CHILE
The highest volcano in the world.

APRIL

IMJA TSE (ISLAND PEAK), NEPAL
Often used as a "training peak" by people wanting to climb Everest.

JUNE

DENALI, ALASKA
The highest peak in North America.

JULY

MONT BLANC, FRANCE
The highest mountain in the Alps.

AUGUST

MATTERHORN, ITALY
This striking peak is a near-perfect pyramid shape, with four distinct sides.

OCTOBER

MERU PEAK, INDIA
The "Shark's Fin" route up this mountain is one of the world's hardest climbs.

NOVEMBER

AORAKI/MOUNT COOK, NEW ZEALAND
The highest mountain in New Zealand.

DECEMBER

PICO DE ORIZABA, MEXICO
This active volcano is the highest mountain in Mexico.

MOUNTAIN WORDS

ADAPTATION When a type of animal or plant becomes well suited to a particular habitat, often by developing particular characteristics or features to help them survive.

ALTITUDE How high up something is from the ground or sea level.

AVALANCHE A large amount of ice, snow, or rock falling quickly down a mountainside.

CANYON A deep, narrow valley with steep cliffs on either side, often with a river or stream running through it.

CONIFER FOREST Forests that are mostly formed of conifers, which are a group of trees and shrubs that produce cones and have needle-like leaves.

ECOSYSTEM A community of living things and their environment.

FAULT LINES Long cracks in the Earth's crust.

FOOTHILLS Low hills at the base of a mountain.

FOSSILS Preserved remains of animals or plants that lived long ago. They are often found buried in rock.

GEYSER Rare springs that shoot fountains of hot water and steam from underground.

GLACIER A thick mass of ice that flows incredibly slowly downhill, like a river.

HABITAT The natural environment where an animal or plant usually lives.

HOT SPRING A spring of naturally hot water, heated by volcanic activity underground.

ICEFALL Jagged blocks of broken glacier.

MOUNT EVEREST
Highest summit in the Himalayas (and the world!)
29,031.69 ft above sea level

MOUNT KILIMANJARO
Highest free-standing mountain
19,340.55 ft above sea level

LAVA Hot, liquid rock that flows out from volcanoes or cracks in the Earth's crust.

LOWLAND An area of land that is lower than most of the land around it.

MAGMA Hot, liquid rock that flows below the Earth's crust.

MOORLAND An open area of land containing hardy shrubs and grasses, where few trees grow.

MOUNTAIN RANGE A group or line of mountains connected by high ground.

MOUNTAIN SYSTEM A group of interconnected mountain ranges.

PEAK The pointed top of a mountain.

SEA LEVEL The average level of the sea where it meets land. The height of a mountain is often calculated in relation to sea level.

SNOW LINE The level or altitude of a mountain above which snow is found for all or most of the year.

STALACTITES Spikes of rock that hang from the ceiling of a cave.

SUMMIT Another word for the top of a mountain.

TECTONIC PLATES Large pieces of the Earth's crust.

TREELINE The level or altitude above which no trees grow.

UPLAND An area of high or hilly land.

VOLCANO An opening in the Earth's crust through which lava, volcanic ash, and gases erupt (escape). Most volcanoes form into a hill or mountain.

MONT BLANC
Highest summit in the Alps
15,766.37 ft above sea level

MOUNT ELBERT
Highest summit in the Rocky Mountains
14,439.63 ft above sea level

INDEX